INDELIBLE SHADOW

poems by

Sandra Berris

Finishing Line Press
Georgetown, Kentucky

INDELIBLE SHADOW

Publisher: Leah Huete de Maines
Editor: Christen Kincaid
Cover Art: April Pacheco
Author Photo: April Pacheco
Cover Design: Elizabeth Maines McCleavy

Order online: www.finishinglinepress.com
also available on amazon.com

Author inquiries and mail orders:
Finishing Line Press
PO Box 1626
Georgetown, Kentucky 40324
USA

Contents

Your body enriches the earth
Your soul soars free as a bird

IF ONLY

If only you had been on the train
You would have felt its rocking

The hypnotic sway and swooshing
Sounds soothing your dread

Silencing dark thoughts
Bringing instead new dreams

Possibilities in an elusive future
But the train was fast

Challenging you in real time
When the mind

Snapped like a horse's leg
And the boy now broken

Stepped onto the tracks

THE MOTHER

Visitors take
A long last look

Where the body
Fills the length

Of his final house
Each time the mother

Rises from the front row
And leans across her son

She wails loud as a train
As we share her despair

Contemplating the unknowable
Searching for answers

Where there is no know

THE FATHER (1)

The father grills the girlfriend
Again and again

What did he say   Tell me
You must know something

As she sits dumbfoundered numb
In her own grief and shock

Give me the thorns
Along with the roses

He says asking again and again
Tell me anything he said   Tell me

As if she keeps a secret
As if anyone could know

THE FATHER (2)

The father looks over the room
Full of mourners who squeeze

Inside the chapel uninvited
An invasion of students and teachers

Coaches and neighbors
Who need to share in this loss

The private service delayed
As an unending line of teens

Pass by the casket's waxy figure
This popular handsome gifted boy

They weep and exit to let others in
And then the father stands to speak

Says my kid was an amazing kid
Was a great kid that little shit!

His anger sheds dewfall
On everyone present

LITTLE SISTER

The darling little sister says
My brother is dead

Just four years old   So young
To declare profound knowledge

Mommy says we all will die
My brother is dead

When will I die, she asks
Where did my brother go

Where is heaven
Can I go see him

My brother is dead
Will he be home for my birthday

My brother is dead
I want him home for my birthday

TRIGGERS

With acrobatic precision
We learn to suffocate sorrow

Never say train
Never say death

Never say suicide
Especially never say suicide

One can lead to another
On this fragile tightrope

She has lost
Part of herself

The two were entwined
And defined each other

More than self
With the other

Now the video of his life
Streams on the wall

Where he smiles
Playing the piano

Kicking soccer goals
Holding a sign

U + Me = Prom?
And there is no fast forward

FORESHADOW

They say if you look back
You turn to salt

That day we saw you
Seated at the kitchen counter

Hunched over schoolwork
One hand, your left

Worrying your hair
A bulk of black

Until rearranged
In an ominous chunk

The expression we mistook
For studious so we

Left you alone
Didn't bother to ask

If you were all right
Took your silence

As serious business
Purposeful intent and

When you rose to go
You barely whispered

Got to go
And disappeared

Into the late afternoon
Leaving us to revisit

This day when we taste salt
Our tongues pierced

With a thorn of regret

HOPE

On her bedroom wall
A dead boy smiles

In a charcoal drawing
His dark eyes shine

Beneath a bolt
Of jet black hair

His wide dimpled smile
So near her once-happy face

This keepsake for remembrance
Now of love and loss

And close to her heart
A new tiny tattoo

A yellow bird transcending
This new space between them

As month by month   one breath at a time
Her self rebuilds

She quotes Martin Luther King
We must accept finite disappointment

But we must never lose infinite hope

TRAINS

Each night nearby
Trains rumble like thunder

She closes windows
Locks her bedroom door

She closes her heart
Afraid to bleed again

(THIS PAGE IS BLANK)

Go back
The blank page is for you

Fill it with sorrow
Record all special moments

What begins
Must also end

STOP
Erase

The page is blank
Write a different version

After every end
Is a beginning

CHINESE FAREWELL

You were smart as the rat
Gentle as the rabbit
Playful as the dog

By your headstone we bow
And put our fists together
In respect

We send lanterns to heaven
So our dreams may come true—
Fly high yellow bird

THE LEFT FOOT

After W.C. Williams

so much depends

upon

the left

foot

amidst a winning

soccer team

for a bright

future

THEN

If
The left foot is magic
Maneuvering the field

If
The team is winning
Attracting scouts

If
The offers are competitive
Vying for the foot

If
The future depends
Upon the left foot

If
The foot is injured
Creating doubts

Then

GREEN

Hand in hand in hand
You he and baby sister

Walked through spring flowers
In the high meadow

Above the highway
A favorite place

Where yellow flowers abound
In the green of spring

Green   his favorite color
And now yours and mine

BRAIN PUZZLES

Why does a squirrel run
Halfway across the street

Why do birds fly
Into window glass

What makes a fish flip
Out of a bowl

Can something be hidden
In plain sight

Why does a boy step
In front of a train

Can a scream be so loud
It can't be heard

IT IS OKAY

You may weep.
Grief is real.

And though you feel
Alone, grief is common

And sorely felt. Right now
You are at an end

But it is not the end.
You will feel more grief

(Not news you care to hear)
But you will also feel joy

So unimaginable at this moment.
Yet joy is chosen

And soon you will look at the sky
Full of stars and smile

At their glint in the darkness,
Or marvel at the many shades

Of blue in the ocean, its constant current
Never running dry. Dare you

Look outside at that hummingbird
Suspended in the air, the miraculous

Beating of its wings. You too
Will navigate the world in a new way

Rebuilding your sense of wonder.

With Thanks

Thank you to Finishing Line Press for selecting my chapbook for publication, with special thanks to my editor Christen Kinkaid, to Kevin Maines, publisher, and to the staff whose attention to detail and design are much appreciated.

Many thanks to April Pacheco, artist, photographer, and professional businesswoman extraordinaire, whose creative spirit clicked immediately when I mentioned ideas for a cover design. Her drawing of the yellow-tinted bird inspired the title *INDELIBLE SHADOW*.

Much gratitude to Joanne Dearcopp for sharing her publishing and editing acumen and for encouraging me to create this chapbook of highly personal poems.

Heartfelt appreciation of my loving family who understands that writing is central to my emotional processing and my interaction with the world around me and gave me permission to print these poems. We share the difficult search for a continuous healing path.

Thank you to Ohana Montage Health of Monterey County that specializes in the mental health of young people. Their ground-breaking work in serving the teens of Monterey County, California, helps others to recognize when to seek professionals for deserved support.

And last, but so significant, thank you to my husband, Brian, for his perpetual willingness to read drafts of my poems, his keen suggestions, and loving encouragement.

Sandra Berris was born in Chicago, but grew up in Lincoln, Nebraska, where she earned a B.S. from the University of Nebraska and began creative writing under Karl Shaprio, a Pulitzer Prize winning poet, who taught her, "You can't write about life unless you mean the magazine or the cereal," i.e. be specific. She served as co-editor of Professor Shapiro's annual magazine of students' poetry and fiction.

She next earned her M.A. in Education from Stanford University and was an English teacher for several years before moving back to Chicago. There she became co-founder and editor of *WHETSTONE* Literary Magazine that garnered eleven National Endowment for the Arts/Illinois Arts Council Literary Awards over its eighteen years of existence.

A group of her poems received a Hugh J. Luke Poetry Prize awarded by Prairie Schooner and her work was anthologized in *Best of Prairie Schooner* (University of Nebraska Press, 2001). Her work has been reprinted and anthologized in magazines and books including *Chicken Soup for the Soul: Family Caregivers and Storms of the Inland Sea, poems of Alzheimer's and Dementia Caregiving*.

Other recognition includes: finalist for the Randall Jarrell Poetry Prize 1996, finalist for *Inkwell's* Poetry Competition 2001, Honorable Mention for Nonfiction for *New Millennium Writing* Awards XVIII, 2005, finalist for "The Look of Love" 2007 International Poetry Competition.

She is a member of Authors Guild, PEN America, the Academy of American Poets, Poetry Society of America, and Greenwich Pen Women, a branch of the National League of American Pen Women.

Her first book-length collection of poems is *Ash on Wind* (Muse Ink Press, 2017). A sample of these poems can be found at www. SandraBerris.com

She lives in Carmel-by-the-Sea, California, where she enjoys daily beach walks, plays golf while simultaneously watching for spouting whales, plays bridge, and writes poetry.

.